Dora's Poems

Dora Jones Fisher

A publication of

Eber & Wein Publishing

Pennsylvania

Dora's Poems

Copyright © 2017 by Dora Jones Fisher

All rights reserved under the International and Pan-American copyright conventions. No part of this book may be reproduced, stored in a retrieval system, or transmitted in any form, electronic, mechanical, or by other means, without written permission of the author.

Library of Congress
Cataloging in Publication Data

ISBN 978-1-60880-586-0

Proudly manufactured in the United States of America by

Eber & Wein Publishing
Pennsylvania

This book is dedicated to my mother Mattie C. Washington Jones, who inspired me to write.

She loved to write but did not get a chance to follow her dreams.

To my husband Melvin C. Fisher Sr., my children Melvelyn, Melvin Jr., and Mya Fisher—

I love them so dearly.

Acknowledgements

I want to thank God for giving me the desire and strength to write this book.

I want to thank my sister Margie Jones, Eber & Wein Publishing, and all who encouraged me to keep on writing.

Thanks to my mother-in-law Bessie Davis.

Thanks also to my sister-in-law and brother-in-law Geraldine and Vernon Cromedy, who have always inspired me to be the best at whatever I do.

Thanks to all my family.

Many thanks to Canaan Missionary Baptist Church of Little Rock, Arkansas, and Pastor D. A. Witcher, for allowing me to share my poems with them.

A Kind Man

There is a man who is as kind as can be
He sits in his backyard working up under the trees

In his own world working away
He works with his hands working all day

He always takes time to listen to a friend
He listens from beginning to end

All in his world he seems very pleased
Sitting there working up under the trees

A Kind Woman

When I met Karen for the very first time
I could tell she was so very kind
When we spoke I felt that she would be a good Christian friend
After meeting her way back then
I did not know we would cross paths again

It wasn't too long; we worked side by side
And with our little talks I realized

What she carries inside and does not mind sharing
Is a sweet spirit in her everywhere she goes
Everyone knows
Christ is in her life and there is no mistakin'
She loves our Maker

I believe God knows what her pure soul holds
And I know its weight is more than a pot of gold
Like everyone else, she has had some times when she needed to cry
But I never saw a tear in her eye

And when she had her pain, I never heard her complain
She just prayed and called on His name
She is as sweet as can be; if you meet her you will see
She is a true Christian and you can tell
Because she shows it so very well

She is very special because I believe she is chosen by the Lord
As one of His vessels to let people know that He loves them so
And He will understand
If they give Him their hand

We met that season for a reason
It was in His plans
He knew that she would be faithful and understand
Jesus knew Karen through and through
And if chosen by Him, she would help make one of my dreams come
    true

Because of her love for Jesus Christ
And her love for her sisters and brothers
I believe she is bound
To receive and wear her crown

A Man Named Tim

If you meet a man as nice as Tim
You should get to know him
Because he is as precious as a gem

Life is never dim when you know a man like Tim
If you need him he is not very far
He will be there for you wherever you are

He picks his friends and he picks them well
He can tell if you would be a true pal

He does love his music
He can sing most anything
He sings, plays the piano and guitar
Just like a music star

With his music he is led by the spirit to bring in souls
Rich, poor, young, and old

Most of all, he is a man of God; this he does not have to think twice
God is first in his life, and to him that is the best advice

You can tell he loves and trusts God because he shows it in his heart
And there you can feel Jesus right from the start

As Time Goes By

As time goes by, you stop and think to yourself, oh my
How the time has gone on by with just one blink of an eye

One day you are playing with your friends and your toys
Making lots of noise

Running, playing, laughing in the streets
Till your legs get so weak right down to your feet

So very neat to have that much fun
Back then you stayed out with the sun

When it went down
We knew it was time to finish our rounds

'Cause it was the start
Of the break of dark

And of course by then you were tired
Especially when you would start having fun
At the crack of dawn

Dora Jones Fisher

Beauty of the Trees

It is so amazing how the trees are so at peace
They stand there looking at me

When the rain comes
They just stand in the wind and cold
Getting so wet
Taking it all, I bet

How do they do it?
Some being so skinny and tall
So frail and old
But they still stand there so very bold

In the fall when the leaves turn colors and die out
They become so beautiful and stout

We should be like the trees in the fall
When we leave this world and all
We then should look so beautiful in the end

Beyond the Sky

I would lie in my backyard in the green grass
Looking up in the sky seemed so odd, seemed like glass

I wondered if anyone knew
How it could be so pretty and blue

I wanted to see so far up in the sky
I wanted to see beyond where Mom said you go when you die

Stretching my eyes so wide
Wanting and hoping that I may see what is up there all inside

Sometimes when the sun is too bright
I just close my eyes so tight

I love to lie in the green grass
So soft and plush and it felt so luxurious

With the sun on my skin, the grass so cool and thick
I could fall to sleep quick

I would think to myself, are you there?
I know you are there somewhere

Most of all I tried and tried to see beyond the sky
Hoping that I could stretch my eyes and see so far

Are you way up there in the sky?
Oh how I want to say hi
So I lie back, look up, and know that someway and somehow
I will see one day beyond the sky

Dora Jones Fisher

Black History Week

I just love Black History Week
To me it is so neat

We get to talk about, men, women, boys, and girls
People who made some great accomplishments all over this world

What makes it so special is we get to learn
About people like you and me who decided to follow their dreams
They were blessed to achieve their best
The desire they held inside, I believe, was guided by God

Someone asked me, should we celebrate Black History Week?
Oh yes, we must indeed
There is a lot of history that we still need
To let our children know because of others and their deeds
We, too, can succeed

We need to know about some of our great achievers
Especially the ones who went above and beyond
Even in Arkansas we have some outstanding leaders
To make their mark

But to top it all
Another one of the greatest histories of all
Is the swearing in of our president and first lady
Barrack and Michele Obama

We celebrate this day also to learn what they had to endure
They did it for us so we would be secure
And because of their history we can have *victory*!

We truly want to remember these great servants of God
Who loved all people enough to stand and sometimes risk their lives
And fight for what was right

Black History belongs to all people, I am told
Black and white, men and women, young and old

This day is set for us to learn from each other
And be proud of our great sisters and brothers
And know that because they paved the way for us
We can hold our heads up today and rejoice!

Dora Jones Fisher

Bosses

Some bosses are nice
And will give you good advice

Some bosses are just plain-old mean
And will make you do everything

Some stand over you like a guard
And some are just too hard right from the start

Some are in and out, all about here and there
Some are very nonchalant and just don't care

But if you get a boss who will treat you fair
Hope and pray he will stay there

Brother, Brother

Brother, brother, what's the matter?
He has fallen into a deep, deep sleep
Won't you please wake up? What will it take?

You are there; can you hear me?
For you lie there in peace

Brother, brother, fight for your life
Can't you see it's between you and Him?

He has given you lots of chances
To change your life and make you complete

This time now it is up to you
I believe He is thinking what He is going to do with thee

Get your rest
He is grading your test
He will decide and He won't guess

Till then, dear brother, go on and get your rest
Whatever He does, it will be for the best

Cry

Little girl, little girl, my, my
Why are you crying?

What could make that rosy face cry?
So sweet and tender
Young and dear

Cry, cry, cry
Little girl, why?

Dry your tears and listen here
Whatever it may be
Just remember, you see

Forgive and forget
Learn and be wise

Wipe your eyes
And don't be surprised

It's a new day
So go on and play

Daddy, I Miss You

When you were here I never got to say
How much I love you from day to day

Not in the morning and not even in the noon
Never did I think you would leave us so soon

One day I looked for you and you were gone
You were like a tree standing so firm and strong
Never did I think you would ever leave us alone

Daddy I miss your big old arms
That wrapped around us and made us so warm

I will always remember the Christmases you shared
Daddy I know you really cared

It was magical, mystical, exciting, filled with joy
That is what you brought to us with a brand new toy

Lord we were poor and poor as can get
But never, never, never did Daddy ever quit

You put a smile on our face
That will never get erased

One thing I believe in my heart
God knows how he worked so hard

It had to be rough and it had to be tough
To make sure that it was enough

One thing I know from child one to child ten
We loved our daddy from beginning to end

Dora Jones Fisher

Daddy Went Home

When we embraced
I knew something was wrong
Something was wrong when we embraced face to face

When we held each other
I felt his chest against my breast
It felt as hard as a brick
And that I will never forget

He said goodbye
Without even moving an eye

I wanted to not let go
And I walked away moving kind of slow

As we drove up on the interstate
He waved his arm
And it looked as if he was raising a ton of weight

We waved goodbye; he looked a little sad
And I said I hope this is not the last time I see old Dad

After a couple of days the phone rang while I lay in bed
I said, *Is it Dad?*

I knew with fear
When I saw my husband's eyes filled with tears

I already knew why
Because that was the first time I saw him cry

Big raindrop tears ran down his face
I already knew; I already guessed
That Daddy went home to rest

Daughter

Oh, daughter, my sweet daughter
What is this?
Your eyes filled with tears streaming down your face
Oh, my dear, don't you know I am here?

I know it gets hard to bear, and at times you say why
Oh, my daughter, no need to cry

Remember, I was spit on and laughed at
As I walked through the streets
People wondered, who is this man?

Starving to teach what I knew for years
My twelve disciples held their fears
As they walked with me to share my love
That came from above

As I was spun around from head to waist
With that crown stuck in my brow, I felt the blood run down my face

My body ached with pain for every nation
As I pressed my way again through the street to meet my destination

With my arms stretched wide
Blood streamed down my side
This was not false
My child, I hung there on the cross

I looked up to the Father and I asked him to forgive them
For they knew not what they did
I hung on the cross, not for a fee
But all to set you free

My sweet, dear daughter, don't you cry
For I am here; I will always be here
So dry your eyes and don't you cry

Dora Jones Fisher

Dear Mother

Into this world I came
Being spit out of your womb

I screamed of rage filled with fear
From leaving what I cherished so dear

Placed upon thy breast I lay
Dear God, you prayed
Thank You for this child You gave

Still shaking from leaving my beautiful nest
You bent down and kissed me granting my only request

You took me home
I was never alone

Even when I was sick and shook with fear
By my side you were near

You taught me right from wrong
You taught me how to be strong

You were as wonderful as can be
Thank you, dear Mother, for loving me

Do You Love That Dog Better Than Me?

Honey do you love that dog better than me? I can tell
You treat him so well

I don't love him better than thee, but I do love him
Because when he sees me he wags his tale

He doesn't complain when I bring him his food
He is so happy and in a good mood

And he is there to greet me when I am at the door
With warm kisses he seems to enjoy

Always glad to see me however long I am gone
He will sit there and wait till I get home

Even if I don't have a bone he doesn't care
He still waits for me right by my chair

When he plays with his favorite toy
He always invites me to play with so much joy

He never complains about anything I do
He's always so happy to see me all fresh and renewed

And that is really, really so unlike you; of course I love you more
But him I truly adore

Dora Jones Fisher

Don't Walk on the Sidewalk

As we sat under a tree, my sister said
Let me tell you what happened back in 1957
My friends and I would walk home together after school
It was the rule
All seven of us—three girls and four boys
We had no choice

This particular day because the traffic was so busy
The boys told us girls, we are going to walk on the sidewalk

We were a little afraid because our parents told us we better not
But the boys talked us into it anyway
They said, be quiet, walk fast, and make no noise
I thought to myself, oh those crazy boys

As we walked and talked, the first tomato and egg hit our head
We thought we were dead
Then we heard white people calling us names
What a shame
Then we knew it was not a game

Our boys threw back some tomatoes
And someone called the police
We took off running, I dropped my brand new books
So I had to go back

As I bent down to pick them up, I looked up
There was this policeman standing over me
Shouting, *halt*, and he was holding a gun in his hands
Pointing at my head; it scared me so bad I wet my pants

They took us to jail
As we road in the police car we were teased

And they tried to scare us all
We spoke up and said
When Daisy Bates and NAACP find out about this
You might lose your jobs

They took us inside the jail
We were between the ages of eleven and twelve
And I must say as of today
I don't ever want to be treated that way

Our parents came as fast as they could
When they stepped inside
I opened my eyes wide
I was so glad to see my mom and dad

I said to my parents, you would have been proud
Of us, what we said and now
I know why you told us not to walk on the sidewalks
And I hope and pray
Things will change someday

Dora Jones Fisher

Fresh Peaches

Have you ever reached up and picked a peach?
All you have to do is reach
Up and take it right off the tree
To pick a peach it is so neat

Makes you feel so at ease
When you pick a peach
If you would take a bite
With all your might
It tastes so good
Like it should

You don't need a knife
Just take a bite
It tastes so sweet and juicy to me
Oh how I love those fresh peaches

Fresh peaches are the best compared to the ones in the store
Fresh peaches will make you go back for more

Girl, Stop

Girl, stop
Just stop all that worrying for nothing
Stop

Now start living put it aside
Come back to it another day
It won't be long
It won't take long

What you want and can't get right now
Ain't going to get you nowhere

Stop, stop, stop and rest your mind
It's working overtime and you ain't
Got a dime

Wasting your time
Put it at the back of the line

Child, you look sick
You got what they call worrying eyes

I can tell you talking slow as a turtle
Get yourself together

Change those eyes with a smile; get wise
And you will be surprised

God Did It All

Why can't they see that God made it all?
If you look around
And even if you go down
Below the sea

So explicit no man can conceive
Below and top
He made it all

What man could have reached so high
To make the sky?

Way beyond is Heaven
Filled with some of His greatest creations

If we think this was magnificent
Just wait and see
What He has just for you and me
I tell you God did it all

Hats

When I was a little girl
I would put on Momma's hats
I thought I was
The most beautiful girl in the world

I loved hats
And when I had one on my head
I thought I was all that

I would put my hand on one hip
And strut my stuff
And Momma would say
Okay, lady, that is enough

You couldn't tell me anything with my hat on
In my mind I was somebody
When I would walk past you
I would hold my head up

Yes, I became a gracious queen
And oh how I would beam
I love hats and hats were my thing

Dora Jones Fisher

How Small Are Your Feet?

Look at those little feet
They look so small to me

How small are your feet?
Size one, size two, size three?

How do you walk on the street
With those little bitty feet?

They are so small to me
Just tiny as can be

They make me giggle when you wiggle
Stick out your feet so I can tickle

Let me figure
I must say my baby's feet are bigger

Stick out your toe
So I will know
How neat
And pretty are your feet

I Am Just Sleeping

Lord, I lie here in the hospital bed
They say they thought I was just about dead

For days I took a journey
I crossed the ocean and the seas
I drifted through the air
And I did not go anywhere

It was no one but me
I had to be brave and not afraid
In fact I was ready because I study His word

So I waited on my own
Locked in my body
People above me
Calling on Your name, praying and praying

I was ready
But You woke me up
Not sure why, but You did
And now I know

You are keeping me here for a good reason
So I can say no need to weep
I am just sleeping

I Am So Happy God Has Blessed Me

I am so happy with what God has done for me
I am so happy to know He knows me

He blessed me once and He blessed me twice
I am so happy with what He's done for me
I am so happy with what He's done for me

One day when I was weak and worn
Didn't know which way to turn
He picked me up and made me strong
Set my feet on higher ground

I am so happy with what God has done for me
I am so happy He has set me free
I am so happy, happy as can be

Glory, glory, hallelujah; glory, glory, hallelujah
I am so happy, happy as can be
Glory, glory, happy as can be

I am so happy, so happy
Can you see?
I am so happy

The Lord has blessed me
He blessed me once and He blessed me twice

I am so happy the Lord has blessed me
Glory, hallelujah, the Lord has blessed me

I Can't Read

I tell you I do not want to read
But you said you must indeed

How I wanted to tell you then why
But you still insisted I try

My heart is beating so fast
It was my chance at last

I looked around and in my mind
I was saying can't they see
I am afraid as can be?

Oh they will tell that I can't read very well
Won't they stop? Won't they quit?
They will know that I am illiterate

I Just Did Not Know

I feel so bad I did not know what I had
One day I got a large cut on my leg
It was the length of an egg
But somehow it looked so big to me
So big that people would see it right below my knee
Where my dress or skirt would be

People would say, you have the prettiest legs
But what happened? And they would beg
To touch it, and it felt like they were sticking in a peg

I felt so maimed
Although it was only a cut on my leg, people made me feel so lame
Till one day God opened my eyes
He made me realize that I had to break the ties
That made me want to hide

Oh how I was surprised that I wasted some of my life
Just because of a cut below my thigh that made me cry
And so very shy, I did not know
Till God showed me Mr. Joe
And Mr. Ball
They had no legs at all
My cut, then, seemed so small and slim
Compared to them

How bad I felt because I let everything go
Because of a little cut and because people teased me too much
I know now what I could have had
And I feel so bad I let my dreams pass

I pray God will forgive me
I just did not know
How He blessed me so
My eyes were closed
Perhaps till I would know
And understand most of all
Mr. Joe and Mr. Ball

When I met my husband he had the same cut
But it was on his arm and he had a bandage
Covering it up, I pulled it off
I already knew what he went through
I believe God marked us
So we would meet and begin a life
Together as husband and wife

I Love the Snow

Way back then when it used to really snow
And the snow would stick
It would start in the evening and last all day and night

It was so beautiful we would sit and watch it fall down slowly
Sometimes it would come down fast
We just hoped it would last

I could always tell before it snowed
I could tell by its smell so crispy, fresh, soft, and cold
If you take a deep breath it feels like methanol
Going up your nose

Blow it out, see it come out
Like smoke white as snow, so crunchy
When your feet fall down deep

You can have lots of fun, you know
Playing in the snow
When you slide and run
Make a snowman
Roll the snow, make a big ball
And try to take it all

The sun shining on the snow makes it glow
It dances with sparkles that will dazzle your eyes
It is so beautiful
I love that wonderful snow

I March On

Each day I march toward tomorrow
Each day I do not know
But I still press on with the will of God on my side

I wander through the mist of life
Using the comfort and joy I need to endure
My eyes are closed as I pray on my knees
Lord, please grant our plea

With a pace in my heart the fear makes it race
But I hope they know it's not just for me
Oh I hope they will see that it's not just for me

As I march on I have in my heart
While I am being whipped, spit on, and beaten
Jesus was never defeated

In my mind I will never forget
Jesus held on and never quit
Being beaten, kicked, spit on through and through
All He asked was Father forgive them for they know not what they do

I have learned to hold to my indignation
My strength comes from our Savior
So I still march on with Him in my heart
This is truly my inspiration

I embrace myself now
I can stand with faith and dignity with my chest
Stuck out, I march strong and confident
Not fearing what I will face

Dora Jones Fisher

Wanting what Jesus sacrificed for us so many years ago
When He hung His head and died
And three days later He opened His eyes again to rise

Still we have to fight for our God-given right
Oh freedom, oh freedom
Freedom for you and me

I march on each day
Hoping and praying that our children will know
What our fathers and mothers had to overcome
Not just for me but for all humanity

Life Will Pass You By

As life goes by don't close your eyes
You'll miss it as life goes by
Don't be shy

Time is spinning so fast
For you it will never last
Only for one thing for life

Will it ever end going so fast?
Will it leave you in the past?

What is that you try to do, will you do it alone?
Can you do it before the day is gone?

Tell me, what is that you do?
Will it do you any harm?
Will you do it till it is done?

Oh my life will pass you by fast as an apple pie
Don't ask why

It won't leave you alone till it is through spinning
It's cycle over and over
Quick and swift it's there
Then it is gone
Oh my, life will pass you by

Dora Jones Fisher

Little June

There was this boy who lived up the street in a little white house
We would call and call for him to come out and play some basketball
Till one day we found out he could not hear at all

Soon he started coming out to play but only in the afternoon
His mother said it is the only time you could play with Little June

I wondered why they called him Little June
But we didn't care 'cause we loved to play with him
Even only in the afternoon

He was so nice to us when we would play
Then one day he moved away
We wished he had not moved so soon
'Cause we missed him, our Little June

Little Kitty

I had a little kitty
She grew up with me
We would sit on the back porch early in the morning
I brushed her coat and made her look so pretty

We were best friends, and she was kind as could be
But one day she grew up and had a family

As the days passed by
Little kitty got too busy for me to rub her coat
I could plainly see

But she would still come
And wrap her coat around my legs
To let me know
That she still remembered and truly loved me so

Dora Jones Fisher

Mother, Do You Know My Name?

Mother, do you know me? Oh, Mother, who am I?

You knew me in your womb
With every move, you cherished
You knew me as I entered into this world
So very, very scary

With your warm smile so dear
And the love I felt so near
As they placed me upon your heart
I gave out a great cheer
Mother, I know you know me because you calmed all my fears

When I kept you up late at night singing, praying, and pleading
That the Lord would hear your prayers just for little oh me...he

You knew me when I left your arms the very first time for school
As I raised my hand to say goodbye
Oh, Mother, please don't cry
I saw a tear run down your face
Mother, I know it's hard but don't forget how
I kept you up praying to our God

You knew me when it was time to let go; oh boy, that was hard
But you taught me the most important thing of all
To put your trust in God

You knew my children; you shared the same with them
Mother, you knew all your children's, children's, children
And I know you know their names

Now you are old and walking with a cane
Alzheimer's has crept into your veins, trying to steal your flame
Let nothing steal your joy; that is what you taught me thus far

You don't have to know my name still
I will cheer you on, praying and singing to ease your pain
Together we will fight to the bone
Letting Alzheimer's know that we are strong
And God is never wrong

I love you, Mother, and face to face
We will win this race

Dora Jones Fisher

Mr. President and First Lady Obama

Your time has come; all is well and done
Your time has come and gone

What will you do now? Have you thought and planned
How to be a normal woman and man?

You did all you could and to yourself you knew you should
Make this USA a better place to stay

I know you found out it was difficult to achieve
I know you found out a lot and it was hard to believe

But I bid you well and I give you my utmost respect
Because you stood the test that I will never regret

Your persevering and determination never to quit
And to do your best this I will never forget

I will miss you, Mr. President and First Lady, always and forever
It has truly been an honor
To know that you accomplished
One of the greatest achievements in history

And this I will hold in my heart to never part
It shall be there to stay even when I close my eyes and all is dark

Mrs. Mary

Mrs. Mary what is wrong?
I thought you were strong

I thought you were taught to carry on

You know where we come from
It was far more worse than this

Mrs. Mary you must not quit
One thing I want you to not forget

God has some of his strongest soldiers
On the battlefield

When times are so hard
And you can't think or see straight

You feel like things ain't right
And that you still have to fight

Just remember to be strong and hold on tight
Embrace yourself and keep your faith

Be proud and remember do no wrong
I know it is hard

But always remember
You are chosen by God

Dora Jones Fisher

My Husband

I love my husband
He is sweet as can be
I love my husband
He grew up with me

When we met I couldn't tell yet
That he would be the one
I would catch in my net

I loved his nose; it was quite pretty
To me it is long and I like it
He is the one I choose

He is funny with a sweet personality
And I love him because he filled me with laughter

When we would sit and talk
We learned that our parents taught us just about the same
They taught us about a man
And Jesus is His name

We had many things in common
We played the same games

Most of all we both are believers
Love and fear our God

My Son

Son we know you are now a man
I know we wanted to keep
A hold of your hand

You grew up so fast
I bet you thought at last

And we want you to always remember you are our son
We only have one

When you are in need
We are here to hear you plead

If you need us we are here
We will be your cure

I know you are not holding on to my skirt
Anymore but when you need us give it a jerk

You are the one the family will lean on
Son, you won't be alone

All we want you to know
Is we love you so
And we will love you forever, wherever you go

Dora Jones Fisher

My Stomach Ache

Oh my stomach
Something I ate

I got a stomach ache
Must have been something on my plate

How it hurts and feels so bad
It was something I had

Could it have been that sweet, sweet cake?
It will keep me up too late
'Cause I now hear the noise my stomach makes

How long will it take? I am so wide awake
Next time I will watch what I take

Next time I will not eat what everybody bakes
Oh how my stomach aches

Mya on That High Slide

I never thought that Mya would ride the highest slide
She walked all the way up to the top for a ride

How brave she was to walk way up
I hollered, *Mya, that is enough*

But she kept right on up to the top
She never stopped

That little girl Mya was not so shy
To go up so high

When she got to the top step she waved
And a smile she gave
With one push she went down
That Mya is so brave

Dora Jones Fisher

No One Ever Told Me

When I was young no one ever told me about the rules
Exactly why you had to go to school

One day I got sent to the counselor at school
She said you should take a class for the summer
To help you with your curricular

I said to her, for what?
My husband will take care of me for the rest of my life
Thanks for your advice

Now that was a lie, I have proved it to be
I thought I would never have to work a day in my life
And I would be this loving stay-at-home wife

Just like my mother I thought I would be
Back then things were so nice and it did not take a lot to survive

If only someone would have explained this to me
All about the economy
And that you really need to get a college degree

And that he might need me to help him with the family affairs
Or someday my husband might not even be here

Nowadays it is possible you can stay at home
But most of the time he can't do it alone

Now that I know what it takes
I might go back to school
They say it is never too late

O Lord, Forgive Us

Lord, I am so sorry for the way some people are so far
I know we are one of Your very creations

You made one; that's how it begun
Just like that it was done
Then from one it turned into a ton

I know you wanted us to be right in Your sight
And I know that sometimes You held Your might

I think we were highly favored
So thank You for sending Your Son to teach us behavior

You would think that after all these years we would trust
And know that You are among us

And that should make us feel so very blessed

Dora Jones Fisher

One Day I Had a Dream

One day I had a dream it was so real it seemed
In my dream I could see
A city come down right out the sky

It was a warm feeling, felt so assuring to me
But also hard to believe what my eye could conceive

Inside this city was a building amazing to see
With a pointed round top it was all covered in pure gold

Right in the center of this city was a man standing
Behind a pulpit dressed in white and he wore a crown

As it came down it did not touch the ground
When I looked around Grandma was there
Standing right in the middle
All in her pretty white gown

It began to snow big flakes that turned into big snow balls
I looked again at Grandma and she looked so
Beautiful and happy as the snow began to fall

When I woke up I thought to myself could it be
What I think I had seen

I called to tell Momma about my dream
She said, "Oh sweet honey, Grandma's work is all done
And to heaven she has gone."

One Word

I always say you never know
When someone is feeling so low

Give them a hug and a smile
Take the time to talk a while
Even if you have to walk a mile

Listen and give them your hand
Let them know you understand

Pray before you choose the words you want to say
Because just one word may change your day

Just one word can be great advice
Just one word can change your life

Dora Jones Fisher

Our Brother

When you were a little boy, you were sweet and cute as could be
Everyone loved to pick you up and hold you in their arms
You had the prettiest eyes and that good curly hair

Yes, we were kinda jealous
Because we thought Mother loved you more
She loved us all the same, but you were her baby boy

When you got old enough to play with us, we had tons of
Fun, running, jumping playing in the dirt
Laughing till our sides would hurt

We also shared our fears together
I know that because you were taught to be a man and be brave
But I knew you were just like me—afraid

Even though you were the youngest one
We cared and protected you for Mom
She would tell us, don't let anything happen to your little baby brother
Yes, you got spoiled not just by mother
But by all of your sisters and brothers

When you grew up and became a man, we knew the path you chose
Was not always fair, but we had to let go

When your eyes closed for the last time here, we were near
And we hoped and prayed that you would understand
We were there for you and never stopped trying to help and love
Our little baby brother

As for me your baby sister, I will miss you the most
After all, we grew up side by side
But I have comfort in knowing that now
Jesus will pick you up and hold you in His arms

Personal Development PD

I walked in my class and sat down in my seat
How I wondered and wondered what PD could be

I looked all around and all I could see
Were people wondering and wondering what PD could be

Our teacher walked in with a smile and she said
My name is Terry you don't have to worry

We will have lots of good fun learning and
Learning what PD can be

She made us all smile and feel at ease
So I sat back in my chair feeling all pleased

She said close the door and sit on the floor
Let's play a game so I can find out everyone's name

From A to Z she taught he and she that PD
Is all about helping you and me

As we left her class we knew in our hearts
She was sharp, oh so sharp

For anyone can have a class
But it takes a special one, you see, who can teach PD

Registration

My sister was silly as can be
Mother asked her to take us to Johnny E. Bush School to register me

This was my first time going to school
I was starting the first grade and all ready for school rules

We walked up some tall, tall steps
It was so much I thought I might need some help

When we walked through the door
My sister took me across the floor
To the table where the teacher began to register four or more

They asked my sister some questions
Then they asked her how old is she
My sister laughed and looked at me
She said she is three and a half going on four, can't you see?

Next thing I knew we were kicked out the door
As we walked down the steps I looked up
And I saw this lady pointing her finger at us

She was mad, mad, mad as can be
She then said with a puff
Don't you ever bring that child back here till she is old enough

When we got home, I told Mother what my sister Mattie did
Mother called Mrs. Burns
She said she is five years old and old enough to learn
Then she made her apologize to Mrs. Burns

Well the damage had already been done
I would have Mrs. Burns as my first grade teacher, oh what fun
Thanks to my sister, that crazy one

Siamese Cat

One day our neighbor gave me a very beautiful cat
She told me to watch out her breed is Siamese
And they are not so easy to please

She also said you must be careful with that kind of cat
You should always know where she is
Because those cats are really smart especially in the dark

I took her home and made her a bed in my dresser drawer
I said to her I will be right back
But when I got back, there was no cat,
I looked and looked all around
And my Siamese cat was gone
I should have never left her alone

I remembered what my neighbor said
"Always know where your cat is"
I called and called, and still no cat
I looked and looked all around even up under every hat
She was nowhere to be found

So I had to get my neighbor to help me find my Siamese cat
She said I told you that Siamese cats are some of the best
And they are so slick
So now please pass me my stick

With all of her experience with cats she knew just what to do
We looked and looked and she said bring me some food and water
Because I cannot find that cat yet

I will go home, you wait a while
When we are gone and all is quiet she will be back
So call me if you still don't find your cat

Dora Jones Fisher

When she does come around
I would suggest you put a collar around her neck
And tie her up, do not worry this you must
Do you see she must get your trust

I waited till after dark then finally she did appear
I said to her, you sweet Siamese cat, you are very smart and so slick

She slid back behind the drawer that I put her in
And I said to my cat
Please don't ever do this again, my sweet little pet

Sneeze

I know a girl at work
All she does is sneeze, sneeze, sneeze

Stop, stop, oh won't you stop with your sneeze

Maybe if you bend your knees
Can you stop your sneeze?

Give her a piece of that cheese
So it will stop her sneeze
Will bees cause her to sneeze?

Oh please, please, please stop your sneeze
I don't believe
How much she has to sneeze

Have you done a good deed?
Lord, would You please bless her to stop her sneeze?

Dora Jones Fisher

Stay the Same

I know some people want things to stay the same
But we must remember things will change
Nothing remains the same

Some of us old folkies feel lost in this world of electronics
And that is not so funny
We can't seem to keep up
We can't seem to learn it quick enough

Computers, phones, televisions, laptops, and desktops
Things are changing so fast in this world—perhaps
That's a lot for us to adopt

Everything now seems
That you have to use the right touch
And that is enough
To make me scream

But when I think of it
I must admit it is not so tough
All I have to do is perfect
My finger to the touch of the screen

Stay Up with Me

When he goes to bed he falls right to sleep
When I go to bed I lie there shaking my feet

He falls into a deep, deep sleep
Why can't I do that—oh no, not me

With my eyes open wide
His snoring is annoying I lie
There in bed
Just looking straight up ahead

I wait and wait
It is very late
By then I have counted all my sheep
And even closed their gate

Whether I am mad or sad he still falls asleep
Even if I weep he still falls asleep

I wish he would sometimes stay up and hold me
I wish he would stay up and say I am here
Have no fear

I wish he would stay up sometimes with me
And I wish he would listen and share our thoughts
Then I will know he really cares and loves me so

I wish he would stay up and wipe away my tears
I wish he would say, I am listening and I love you, my dear

Dora Jones Fisher

Strength in Knowing

Each day I walk toward tomorrow
Each day I do not know but I still
Press on with the will of God

I wander through the mist of life
Using His shield by my side

Believing and trusting in Him
Gives me the comfort and joy
I need to endure

I embrace myself and stand with
Dignity and faith with my eyes closed

As I march strong and confident
And not fearing what I will face

Freely I volunteer, freely I volunteer

Swing, Swing

Swing, swing on the big gum tree
Swing, swing so high

Swing, swing on the big gum tree
I want to touch the sky

Swing, swing on the big gum tree
How high can you go?

Swing, swing on the big gum tree
I surly do not really know

Swing, swing on the big gum tree
Let the wind touch your face

Swing, swing on the big gum tree
Swing, swing oh we swing so fast

Swing, swing on the big gum tree
Let's keep it at a steady pace

Swing, swing on the big gum tree
Feels so good to me

Swing, swing on the big gum tree
Swing and close your eyes

Swing, swing on the big gum tree
Oh my will I touch the sky

Thanksgiving Day

Thanksgiving Day meant so much to me; the house was filled with all kinds of smells of goodies and treats.

My sisters and mom would get up early in the morning to cook our feast. Mom would say you can't wait too late—we have to get started on the pies and cakes.

I got to sleep in because I was the youngest girl but I got up anyway. I couldn't sleep any longer for the smells would wake up my hunger.

We would have so much food; it would last for days. Even though there were ten of us, we still had enough.

One year as we were eating, we heard a knock on the door. Daddy raised up and said I will get it once more.

When he opened the door, a man stood with his hand held out. It was a homeless guy. Daddy came back and started taking food off our plate. I said wait.

Hey, why can't we fix him a plate because it is Thanksgiving today. Daddy said it doesn't matter what I am taking off your plate because he will be more than happy to take it.

I felt sad, but Dad said, be glad because he will be okay. I filled his plate with more than he ever had.

Why do they come to our house every year? Dad thought about it and he said, my dear, it might be your brother telling them to stop by; he, too, is a homeless guy somewhere out there.

The Arkansas River

The Arkansas River so deep and steep
So wide you can't even hide

When you look at it, it looks so calm
You might think it will do you no harm

Its beauty is endless and it stretches
For miles and miles

You can have fun at the Arkansan River
So much fun you will always remember

You can take a walk on the bridge walk
Across and see the edge

But please don't forget if you fall beneath
It's hard to get back upon your feet

Some make it out some may not we must
Respect and don't forget the waters can be
Swift a bit

I took a ride on it one day
Yes it was fun and I wanted to stay

Once you are there it feels so good
So peaceful and so soothing

As the sun shines down on the face of the river
What a show when it glows it makes it look a
Little silver

Oh how I love that old Arkansas River

Dora Jones Fisher

The Beauty of Arkansas

As we travel to Branson, Missouri from Little Rock
There is such a lot of beauty to see

The mountains are up very high sitting there all still oh my
So wonderful and pretty it's all mine for my eyes to see
How amazing something can be so perfectly well designed

When we pass Clinton smooth as a kitten each road we travel is
Up and around nothing like the interstate going just so straight

Around and up we go
Just wait, you can never anticipate what to expect
How exciting it makes you think of your faith

When you are up so high you can look down
Way down to the ground

You are on a mountain
Just breathtaking
Makes your mind flow as a fountain

The meadows so pretty and green, look so clean
This is surely the work of God
And they say they think he did not even work real hard

He did it His way and He did it all and took time
To rest on the seventh day

How marvelous to know that Arkansas our state
Can be so great
I also wonder because Arkansas is so beautiful
If He put a special touch with His hands
When He thought of the Arkansas plans

The Birds and Squirrels

Have you ever looked at the
Birds and the squirrels?
They are all about in this world

Their legs are so swift
When they are about in and out
Without a doubt

Both gather their food
They do it so fast
Sometimes it is done with one quick pick

If you want a squirrel or bird
You have to be quiet and not say a word

So dazzling and fast they are to me
Running playing chasing each other
They are so amazing to see

Dora Jones Fisher

The Birds Fly By

In the morning I love to sit on my porch
Stretch my feet straight out
And with my toes make an arch

I close my eyes and feel the cool fresh
Air then take a deep breath

Then I hear the birds singing everywhere
Just like a great big symphony in the sky

I love to hear the birds singing as they fly by
They sing like we do and it sounds so wonderful

I hear soprano, alto, tenor, baritone
And base, too

Some sing solo some sing with a mate
It sounds so beautiful their pitch is so great

When they sing you could hear a ring
I just love to hear the birds sing

The Clouds

I love the clouds so pretty and white
Sometimes I want to reach out
And touch them with all my might

I love to see what shape the clouds can be
A horse, a cow, a pig, or a rabbit
Oh I have made this such a habit

I love to see the clouds so big and small
Some look soft and some look hard
Some look short and some look tall

It doesn't matter; I love them all
Sometimes they can change
From so pretty and white as a sheet

Sometimes the way they change
Might not be so neat
The clouds can be so frightening and so mean

They can change to a wild, dark, lean
Thunder machine

Their strike can come so keen
I know the clouds can be bitter
Sweet and unforeseen

But I still love looking at the clouds
Because they are so pretty and look so clean

Dora Jones Fisher

The Green Piano

I remember in our house one day we had an upright piano in the middle of the floor
Everyone could see it as they walked through the door

It was green and it seemed so big
It amazed me to know that if you press down
On the keys it would make such a beautiful sound

I wished I could get up on the stool and sit down
But I was too little
And my feet would not reach the peddles

I wanted to climb right up on that big green piano stool using my knees
Just so I can put my finger on those pretty white keys

But still too little I gave up one day
And said I will just listen to my mom play and I pray someday
I will get to play

After growing a little taller I didn't have to worry about my feet
I just walked right in and took my seat

I was going to play like a maestro
Little did I know, the music was wonderful to my ears and I love it so

The next day I happily went in ready to play
I looked up and saw Dad rolling my piano right out the door
He gave it a big push and I saw it fall to the ground
Oh how my heart began to pound

Dora's Poems

I couldn't believe it I had just got old enough to play
And he threw it away
I was so mad at my dad for throwing that big green old piano away
He really, really, really spoiled my day!

Dora Jones Fisher

The House on the Land

As I rode down the highway one day
I was amazed at what I could see
I saw a small house next to some hay

The house was so small, skinny, and tall
Sitting right in the middle of some land
Just like it was sitting in God's hands

Such a strange sight, was it right
I just had to look back again
To make sure it was a house and not a rice bin

I bet whoever lived there had to be little and thin
I thought to myself, is it small
'Cause of the land and all

The only thing that matters is whoever built that house is happy
And it was their plan to build it on all that land

The Key

The way is the key
Enter and it shall be
Done

Lo I come to you
Through each and every
Day

Lo I behold to all
Who may hold

Trust and seek
Trust as it may be

Lo and behold
I have the key

Dora Jones Fisher

The Leaves in the Fall

You can always tell the changing of the season
The leaves will fall with the call of the wind

They go dancing down the streets
Only to meet and greet

With just one gust they jump up together
To make a twirl and swirl up in the air
Making the shape of a volcano as perfect as a pearl

Some just fly up and not make a fuss
Going everywhere so fast in all directions
Some fall in the grass and some keep gliding right on past

How wonderful to see it all
Year after year how the leaves will fall

They change to different colors—orange, brown
Yellow, burgundy, and green
Such a beautiful scene

With one command of the wind the fun will begin
Or will it end and that is all
I love the leaves in the fall

The Light

The way is the light
Enter and it shall be done

Lo I come to you
Through the sight

Lo I behold to all
Who may hold

Trust and seek trust
As it may be

Lo and behold I am the
Light as it is told

Dora Jones Fisher

The Lunch Pail

Daddy got a lunch pail for Christmas one year
He was proud of it and loved it so dear

He used to carry a brown paper bag
When it would rain he would lose the lunch he had

So I guess that is the reason he loved his pail the best
Because it would keep his lunch so good and fresh

On Fridays when he got paid he would fill his lunch pail up
With all kinds of cakes, cookies, and breads
When he came home we would be asleep in bed

He would put his pail on the counter top all filled with a lot
And we would wake up really early in the morning to see who got the pail
It was like a competition to see who would prevail

I would imagine when I looked for his pail that it was a great treasure hunt
Filled with lots of treasures, all you would want

It was such a thrill to whoever got our father's pail
But most of all we shared what we found with each other
And all was well

The Owl

Most of the time when I hear an owl I am in a
Place where all is quiet

I just wait a little while then I hear a hoot, hoot
And I would say oh yes I do, I do hear you

We would mostly hear of owls at night but one
Day my brother and I saw a little baby one

I was so young we had never seen an owl and
We thought he was a creature from outer space

My brother scared that owl so bad he turned his
Head all the way round and fell to the ground
Jumped up and flew away

That owl just did not know that he scared us, too

When we grew up we realized that it was a beautiful
Precious little baby owl and I can't believe he let us get
That close to him for a little while

Dora Jones Fisher

The Rain

I love it when it rains it smells so good
When it falls all on the dry dirt

It will give you such a burst
It will make you very alert

So peaceful always soothing to your skin
Some places it can rain again and again

When the rain comes sometimes you can tell
Before it comes by its smell

It will make you want to yell
And sometimes you can't tell

Rain puts me to sleep
Just to listen as it falls in the street—that is so neat

I love to let it fall all over me so soft, smooth,
Clear, and free I let it get all over my feet

When it falls it can come so fast
How long will it last?

It will make you think
It can be here in a wink

Or it might take days and days but you can bet
It will come at its own pace

I love the rain; it is so for me
I love the rain as you can plainly see

The Trees

How tall you stand so bold and brave
Your toughness is so outstanding
Way beyond the norm
How impressive to see you right there enduring
All the world's chemistry and elements

I love to see you all shapes and sizes
You remind me of the human race
They are small, big, short, tall
But unlike you they can't seem to bear it all

Through the wind, rain, snow, winter, and summer
Still standing so unlike man
This we can barely stand

We can put clothes on us to make us all warm and grand
But I wonder if trees get cold or hot a lot
Can someone tell? Oh, but they do have a bark for a shell
But will it keep them warm?

Some say they are not alive, but I say I feel something inside
I sense their presence
Sometimes I want to cry because of what they have to go through

Something tells me because of the great work they have to do for man
God has a plan for them that someday we will understand

I know the trees were put here for a reason
And I bet it is perhaps to protect us from all the seasons

Dora Jones Fisher

The Wind

Have you ever thought about the wind?
About when it begins and ends?

It blows up, down, and all around
It can even blow on the ground

I have wondered if it is still the same old wind
As the beginning of time

Does it last forever?
Does it have growth or does it age, get tired, and get old?
Who knows? Not us

The scientists have studied and done their tests
And even yet it is still a guess

The wind is just like water
It will never stay in your hands
The wind is light as a feather
When you try and catch it in your hands

But you can gather the wind and it will weigh a ton
If you put it in a pan

One thing I know is the water and the wind
Can be so soothing to the skin

This World

What do I think of this world today?
Well it is changing so much, I must say
If you want to know how so, watch television or go
To the movie show

If you saw the movie *Jurassic Park* you learned all about DNA
And now the investigators use it as of today

If you saw the movie *Enemy of the State*
We learned about some devices that the government can make
To keep up with every move you take
We can now use those tools to protect our schools and estates

What do I think about this world all around us today?

I think it is amazing with lots of new inventions for us to see
But I still say watch television or go to the movie show
So you will see and know some more awesome changes to come

Dora Jones Fisher

Up High Looking Out the Window

At work I stand up high looking out the window at the deer
And I wonder do they know
That people are watching them like a show
The deer play each day running and jumping in the meadow

I wonder do they know they make our eyes glow
With excitement of joy just to see them go?

The grass is very deep, but we still can take a peep
We see them so sweet it makes you want to weep
They are beautiful as can be

Not a care in the world eating, running, and playing
Makes me think to myself if God is looking out His window
Does He see us in that same way?

Unlike the deer we know He sees us and is near
We run and play from day to day

We know He is there at times; I bet some would say
Does He really care?

Even though we can't see Him this feeling I have inside
Tells me He cares and is near

At least we can continue to play
And when we need Him He will be there
Because I can feel Him everywhere

Wake Up, Child

Wake up, child, my darling the dew has fallen
Wake up so you can catch the morning dew

Wake up and go outside today
Before it goes away

Wake up early; don't waste
Let the dew wash your face
Mother would say even today

Wake up, child, early, early in the morning
It will make you feel brand new

It's always good to wash your face
In the morning dew

It makes your face feel all pretty, too
It makes your face feel soft and renewed

It brightens your skin from top to the end
It is different from house water
Wake up child the dew has fallen

Can't you feel the difference on your face
Can't you tell it feels as soft as lace

It is indescribable so please wake up, darling
Wake up, child, the dew has fallen

Dora Jones Fisher

When Daddy Had to Go to Work

In the morning when Daddy had to go to work
Mom would get up early and pack his lunch
She had to fix his coffee that he loves a whole bunch

She had to get up early in the morning
I don't think nowadays anyone would do such a thing

When he went to work in the evening
He would tell her make my coffee very hot
Make it just right because I have to work all night

She would cook a big supper enough to pack his lunch
And then cook him a big breakfast to last till way after brunch

All that cooking she had to do
I say he should have cooked his own breakfast, too

She must have loved that man a lot
To keep his coffee real hot
And fix his breakfast and make so much supper
Just to pack his old lunch box

Who Touched My Face?

Who touched my face?
As I walked by I was so amazed

It was early in the morning in my nostrils
As I took a deep breath

The cool air was so fresh and I felt something
Move across my face

What was it, please?
Was it a breeze?
Felt so good
If you would

It went past my forehead and twirled down my chin
And I asked again

Who touched my face? Some say it was the wind
Was it my kin or was it my friend?

Dora Jones Fisher

Why Can't We See?

At first why can't we know what is
To come

Lord, we make mistakes
Blame each other and ourselves just trying to make
A weight to our expectation

The world is changing before our own eyes
Please don't leave us hanging

We have to wait and try to hold on to
Our faith

We are praying that our love will
Increase

That love will overpower all jealousy
And hate

Lord, would You please help us not to be
Too late for that great, great date

Why Didn't You Tell Us?

Why didn't you tell us about World War II?
You never told us what you went through

Always you showed us how proud you were to serve
I bet it took a lot of nerve

Because of where you were stationed you got to go to many places
How exciting it was for me that you went across the sea

You always taught us to respect and never forget
That you went to fight for our rights

We know you loved your country and were proud as can be
But you never told us the whole story

How courageous and brave you were
You could hear the bombs all above your head
And had to see some of your friends fall dead

You still held on to your gun
Praying that the Lord give you strength to move on

You kept it deep down inside
This you did a good job trying to hide

Till one day I saw you lay your head in Momma's lap and cry
I did not have to ask why
Momma took me by the hand
She said when Dad came home he was a different man

I know Daddy loved the USA
Because he thanked God each and every day

Dora Jones Fisher

We are proud of you and I know you never bragged and cared for
 the attention
But it would not have hurt for you to have mentioned

That you were a sergeant in the army, on your tombstone
It is engraved and I never knew that till I visited your grave

I would have been so proud to know
That you were a leader of some of the most outstanding heroes!

Why Don't They Just Leave Me Alone?

Why don't they just leave me alone?
Can't they see I am just being me?
Because I do not wear my hair like you
And don't keep up with the latest hairdo

Because I do not dress like you
And wear the prettiest outfits like you do
You say I look old, you say it so bold
And you say it so cold
Because my hair is black
With touches of gray everywhere
You say that I look like Grandma May

Why do you look at gray hair as old?
Gray hair can be like silver and gold
When it grows out it comes out white with a beautiful glow
I do not cover this gray hair anymo'
The chemical will take it out for show

Some say my gray is wisdom
And I believe it is a gift from God
You know I'd rather be gray and have some hair
Than to have no hair at all

I know you say get you a wig
Hide all that old gray hair anyway
I am glad you love wearing wigs
I will not talk about you and tell you to let your gray hair grow out
Nor will I tell you that you look bad
I say have fun like you never had

I also say do not worry about me
I am happy as can be

Dora Jones Fisher

Don't worry about my gray hair
I do not need a wig to have fun you see

I am sorry if my hair offends thee
I just want to be me
I know you say I look old
But remember beauty is in the eyes of the beholder

All that matters is what is in my soul
And the one who treats me as precious as gold
When I think of gray hair it reminds me of the song
He washed me as white as snow

Gray hair reminds me of Moses
When he came down from the mount his hair was white as snow
With a glow

I do not care what you think about me
But I do care and hope you can see that I too
Have been washed as white as snow

Do not get me wrong
It is wonderful to look good
So fix your hair, hold your head straight up
If you must and strut your stuff

You Can't Have Too Much of Jesus

You can have too much to drink
You can have too much to eat
You can have so much food that you can't even think

But one thing for sure you cannot have too much of Jesus
He has plenty of food and more

You can have too much perfume
You can have too much cologne
You can have so much that the breeze
Will make you sneeze

Oh yes, one thing for sure
You cannot have too much of Jesus

You better believe it's true
He will fill you up make you feel brand new

Eat as much as you please
There is plenty from Jesus
You do not have to worry if you can have anymore
He will always open His door to give you more

You can have too much of anything
But not too much of Jesus our King

Remember, you cannot have too much of Jesus
He will wipe you clean and fill you up

So do not eat all that other stuff
Come to Jesus He has enough

www.ingramcontent.com/pod-product-compliance
Lightning Source LLC
Chambersburg PA
CBHW031201160426
43193CB00008B/468